THE RULES OF GOLF

according to DENNIS the MENACE

GOLF MENACE

DENNIS THE MENACE AND GNASHER

In 1951, the year Max Faulkner won the Open Championship at Royal Portrush, Dennis the Menace "teed off" as a half-page strip in The Beano — Britain's well-loved children's comic.

With hair like the wildest rough a golfer could imagine, Dennis has an appetite for mischief which would surely make him the number one menace in the world rankings.

In 1968, the year before a Briton next won the Open, Dennis was joined by his now constant canine companion, Gnasher — a hound with teeth so powerful that he crunches the most durable golf balls as if they were peppermints.

Dennis is an enthusiastic convert to the Royal and Ancient game, his Mum and Dad having generously presented him with a set of cut-down clubs.

Generous? Not at all — it's all a clever ruse to allow Dennis's parents a few hours of peace to calm their shattered nerves and clear up the wreckage caused by Dennis.

Dennis and Gnasher invite you to join them for a light-hearted look at the Rules of Golf — a unique chance to laugh and learn.

THE RULES OF GOLF

according to DENNIS the MENACE

with the *reluctant* approval of

First published 2007 by Aurum Press Ltd,
7 Greenland Street, London NW1 0ND
www.aurumpress.co.uk

A catalogue record for this book is available from the British Library

ISBN-10 1 845143 292 0
ISBN-13 978 1 84513 292 7

1   3   5   4   2
2007   2009   2011   2010   2008

Printed in China

CONTENTS

The game of golf continues to grow in popularity, being taken up by thousands of new players each year.

Among those new golfers is the infamous mischief-maker from The Beano comic, Dennis the Menace. Golf is a game of many rules and customs, do's and don'ts, but as Dennis' fans know, Dennis thinks rules are for bending and breaking!

He is a maker of mayhem, a causer of chaos wherever he goes. So when he, accompanied by Gnasher, his partner in crime - and occasional caddie - takes to the course, the result is likely to be outrage and alarm among his fellow golfers.

So why, you may ask, would The R&A of St Andrews -"Home of Golf" and source of the Rules - give its blessing (however "reluctant") to such a work as "The Rules of Golf According to Dennis the Menace"?

Well, first and foremost, this book is meant to be fun. The absurd contrast of Dennis and the game of golf is the first stage. The amazing ways Dennis finds to flaunt, or even rewrite the Rules, is the next.

But through the antics of Dennis and his faithful hound, Gnasher, and also his long-time victims, Walter and the Softies, the attention of golfers - both old and new - are drawn to specific rules with which they should be familiar, as well as some which they may not come across so often.

Beside the Rules, the little anecdotes (true stories every one) from the annals of the Royal and Ancient game serve to show the kind of stuff real golfers are made of. They demonstrate that, no matter what kind of spot you might find yourself in out there on the course, someone somewhere has been in a worse one!

I hope that, apart from giving you fun, this book may help you on the course and even arouse your interest in the Rules!

MICHAEL BROWN
Chairman,
Rules of Golf Committee
R&A Rules Ltd.,
St Andrews

When Arnold Palmer's hooked
second shot landed in a fork in
a gum tree during the second
round of the Masters tournament at
Melbourne, Australia in 1964, Palmer
climbed 20 feet up the tree, hit the
ball 30 feet forward with a one iron,
chipped on to the green and holed
out with one putt.

Rule 1-2. Exerting Influence on Ball

No player or caddie shall take any action to influence the position or the movement of a ball, except in accordance with the Rules.

When professional Carl Hoper hit a wayward drive on the third hole (456 yards) at the Oak Hill Country Club San Antonio during the 1992 Texas Open, he wrote himself into the history books but out of the tournament. The ball kept bouncing and rolling on a tarmac cart path until it was stopped by a fence – 786 yards away.

Rule 2-4. Concession of Match, Hole or Next Stroke

In stroke play you must always hole out. In match play your opponent may concede your next stroke.

The first ever golf shots on the
Moon's surface were played by
Captain Alan Shepard, commander
of Apollo 14, in 1971. He claimed
200 yards with his first shot.
His second was a shank.

Rule 4-4. Maximum Number of Clubs

A player is limited to a maximum of 14 clubs.

A golfer holidaying in Haparanda
in Sweden had a hole in one. The
curious thing is that although he teed
up in Sweden, the green was in
Finland which is in a different time
zone. The time it took for his ball to
travel from tee to cup was one
hour and four seconds.

Rule 6-3. Time of Starting

The player must start at the time established by the committee.

When a team of archers played a
team of golfers over Kirkhill Course,
Lanarkshire in 1953, the archers won
by two games to one. An arrow
landing six feet from the hole, or
a ball three feet, were counted as
holed. Archers whose arrows landed
in bunkers lifted the arrow
and added a stroke.

The responsibility for playing the proper ball rests with the player. Each player should put an identification mark on his ball.

Dr and Mrs B. Rankine playing in a mixed foursome event at the Osmond Club near Adelaide in April 1987, holed in one in consecutive shots, he from the men's with a three iron, she from the ladies with a one and a half wood.

The player must play without undue delay.

Competing in the 1980 Curtis
International Championship Sharon
Peachey drove from one tee and her
ball collided in mid air with one from
another competitor playing another
hole. Her ball ended in a pond.

Rule 6-8. Discontinuance of Play

Bad weather is not of itself a good reason for discontinuing play.

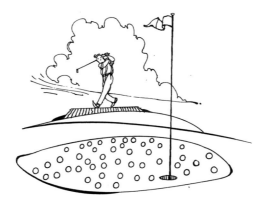

American professional, Harry Gonder, hit 1817 balls over a 16-hour 25-minute period at a 160-yard hole, trying for a hole-in-one. The closest he came to success was hitting the pin once.

In potentially dangerous situations play must be discontinued immediately following a suspension of play.

On a golf course in Uganda there is a sign at one hole which states — "if a ball comes to rest dangerously close to a crocodile, another ball may be dropped for no penalty."

Rule 8-1. Advice

A player shall not give advice to anyone in the competition except his partner.
A player may ask for advice from only his partner or either of their caddies.
(Information on the Rules is not considered to be advice.)

On the glorious 12th of August, the
opening of the grouse-shooting
season, an 11-year-old schoolboy
William Fraser of Kingussie, downed
a grouse with his shot on the
local course.

Rule 8-2. Indicating Line of Play

When the player's ball is on the putting green . . . no mark shall be placed anywhere to indicate a line for putting.

A scratch player and a
high-handicapper played each
other on level terms in a match in the
south of England, the only stipulation
being that the scratch man was to
drink a whisky and soda on each tee.
One hole in the lead, the scratch
man collapsed on the 16th, the
high-handicapper taking the match.

Rule 9-2b. Wrong Information

A player must not give wrong information to his opponent.

Waddy, a beagle belonging to the
secretary of Brockenhurst Manor Golf
Club had found 35,000 balls by the
time it+ had become 11 years old.

Rule 12-1. Searching for Ball

In searching for his ball anywhere on the course, the player may touch or bend long grass, rushes, bushes, whins, heather or the like, but only to the extent necessary to find and identify it, provided that this does not improve the lie of the ball, the area of his intended swing, or his line of play.

Although shut in for three years
surrounded by the eternal snow and
ice of the Antarctic, Arbroath golfer
Munro Sievwright did not neglect
his practice with club and ball. His
luggage included three clubs and
a dozen red-painted golf balls. In
the light of the midnight sun he hit
adventurous shots along the
white wasteland on fairways
of hard-packed snow.

Rule 13-1. Ball Played as it Lies

The ball shall be played as it lies, except as otherwise provided in the Rules.

In the 1927 Shawnee Open, Tommy
Armour took 23 strokes at the 17th
hole. One week earlier he had won
the US Open.

A player must not improve, or allow to be improved, the position of the ball.

F.G. Tait, at St Andrews, drove a ball
through a man's hat and had to pay
the owner 5/- (25p) to purchase a
new one. At the end of the round he
was grumbling to old Tom Morris
about the cost of this particular shot,
when the sage of St Andrews
interrupted him, "Eh, Mr Tait, you
ought to be glad it was only a new
hat you had to buy, and not an
oak coffin."

Rule 13-3. Building a Stance

A player is entitled to place his feet firmly in taking his stance, but he must not build a stance.

In 1955 a player on the Eden course
at St Andrews sliced his drive from
the first tee as a train was passing on
the nearby railway line. The ball went
in through an open window and, a few
seconds later, was thrown back on
to the fairway by a passenger.

Rule 14-1. Ball To Be Fairly Struck

The ball must be fairly struck at with the head of the club and must not be pushed, scraped or spooned.

Two players playing chip shots
simultaneously from opposite sides
of the fairway on the 9th at
Wentworth Falls in Australia were
amazed to see the balls hit each
other in the air above the green . . .
and both fell into the hole!

Rule 16-1c. Repair of Damage to Putting Green

The player may only repair a pitch mark or old hole plug on his line of putt.

During a 24-hour period in November 1971, non-golf-playing athlete Ian Colson played 401 holes over a course in Victoria, Australia. Using only a 6-iron, Colson was assisted by a team of runners who looked for his ball and light at night was provided by a team of motorcyclists.

Rule 16-1d. Testing Surface

During the playing of a hole, a player must not test the surface of the putting green.

Gerald Moxom came straight from a wedding to play in the Captain's Prize competition at West Hill, Surrey in 1934 and, dressed in complete morning suit, went round in 71 to win the competition.

Rule 17-1. The Flagstick

Before and during the stroke, the player may have the flagstick attended, removed or held up.

It took Floyd Rood 1 year and 114 days to golf his way from coast to coast across the U.S.A. The length of the 'course' was 3,397 miles for which Rood took 114,747 shots (including 3,511 penalty shots).

If a player's ball in play moves after he has addressed it, the player is deemed to have moved the ball and he incurs a penalty stroke.

On a damp and low-lying course a
player in a match watched in delight
as his 30-yard approach shot rolled
across the green and disappeared
into the hole. His delight changed into
disbelief when the ball popped back
out a couple of seconds later and
a frog jumped out of the hole.

Rule 19-1. Ball Deflected by Outside Agency

If a ball in motion is accidentally deflected or stopped by an outside agency, it is a rub of the green . . . and the ball shall be played as it lies.

A Brigadier Critchley travelled all the
way from New York to Southampton
and then flew to Sandwich to take
part in the Amateur Championship of
1937 and, despite flying over the
clubhouse to let the officials know he
was there . . . he was disqualified
for being six minutes late.

Rule 19-2. Ball Deflected by Player or Caddie

A player is penalised if his ball is accidentally deflected or stopped by himself, his partner or either of their caddie's equipment.

The seagulls at Pebble Beach are
the world's most brazen birds. On
a daily basis they swoop down and
pluck snacks from the buggies of
unsuspecting golfers. They're
especially attracted to shiny objects.
More than one victim has watched
a gull swoop down, pluck a gold
watch from the buggy, fly away, and
upon realising it's inedible, drop
it into the Pacific Ocean.

Rule 19-5. By Another Ball

If a player's ball in motion is deflected or stopped by another player's ball in motion, the player must play the ball as it lies.

In Ireland's three-week national festival, An Tostal, in 1953, a cross country golf competition, was organised. The golfers played from the first tee of Kildare Club to the 18th green, five miles away, on the Curragh course. Hazards included a railway line, a main road, a racecourse and an army exercise area. The first competition was won by amateur internationalist, Joe Carr, with a score of 52!

Rule 21. Cleaning Ball

A ball on the putting green may be cleaned when lifted.

One of the players in the English
Open Amateur Stroke Play at
Moortown in 1971 overhit his shot
to the last green and the ball
bounced up the steps into the
clubhouse, coming to rest in the bar.
The clubhouse was not out of
bounds, so the player opened a
window and chipped through
it on to the green.

Rule 23-1. Loose Impediments

Loose impediments — natural objects such as stones which are not fixed or solidly embedded — may be removed without penalty.

A local rule at RAF Waddington
reads, "When teeing off from the 2nd,
right of way must be given to
taxi-ing aircraft."

Rule 25-1. Casual Water

Casual water is any temporary accumulation of water on the course but not in a water hazard.

A player once hit a ball towards the 16th green of Combe Wood Golf Club, and the ball landed in the vertical exhaust pipe of a moving tractor. This created a temporary loss of power in the tractor, but when enough compression had built up in the exhaust pipe, the ball was forced out at great speed and eventually landed 3 feet from the pin!

Rule 27. Ball Lost

A ball is "lost" if it is not found or identified within five minutes . . .

In 1929, a husband and wife, whose
house was close to a fairway of a
course in Hampshire, were shocked
when a golf ball came rattling down
the chimney and landed in the fire. A
player's high tee shot had flown out
of bounds and the ball had popped
perfectly into the chimney pot.

Rule 27-2. Provisional Ball

If a ball may be lost outside a water hazard or be out of bounds, to save time, the player may play another ball provisionally as nearly as possible at the spot from which the original ball was played.

In the 1920s a well-known fast
bowler, six feet four inches tall,
arrived at Lords one day with his
chin badly cut and received much
sympathy under the impression he
had been playing on a bumpy wicket.
Not at all. Hitting a tee shot he had
topped the ball so badly that it had
bounced straight up and struck him
on the chin, as violent a blow as he'd
ever delivered an opposing batsman.

Rule 28. Ball Unplayable

The player is the sole judge as to whether his ball is unplayable.

Bill Groves had hit two shots
toward the par-five fifth hole at Dania
Country Club near Fort Lauderdale,
Florida and was planning his
approach to the green when suddenly
a land crab emerged from its hole,
locked the ball in its pincers and
started back down the hole.
Groves also grabbed the ball and a
tug-of-war ensued. The crab won.

Moving a rattling or squeaking cart while an opponent plays a stroke is poor sportsmanship.

In one of the rounds of the News Of
The World Matchplay Championship
in 1960, W.S. Collins and W.J.
Branch were all-square after 18 holes
. . . and it took till the 31st hole to
decide the match, Collins winning. In
1961 in the same tournament, Harold
Henning took 31 holes to beat Peter
Alliss in the third round.

Etiquette. The Putting Surface

Do not drop your golf bag, clubs or any equipment on the putting green.

In a match in 1921 at Kirkfield,
Ontario, P. McGregor needed a long
putt on the last green to win. His ball
rolled up to the lip of the hole and
stopped . . . then a grasshopper
landed on the ball and it fell into
the hole!

Etiquette. Line of Putt

Never step on the line of another player's putt.

When Abe Mitchell and John Ball were playing in the last round of the final of the Amateur Championship at Westward Ho! in 1912, Mitchell's drive to the short 14th hit the open umbrella of a woman spectator and bounced into a bunker. Mitchell was 2 holes up at the time, but lost that hole — eventually the Championship, too, at the 38th.

You should not move, talk, or stand close to or directly behind a player making a stroke.

In a match at Esher in 1931, the club professional, George Ashdown, played each of his shots from a rubber tee strapped to the forehead of Miss Ena Shaw!

No comment should be made to an opponent about his swing during a match.

Spotting a 95-year-old member
slumped in a golf-buggy at Point
Grey Golf Club, Vancouver, a golfer
asked what was wrong. "Heart
failure," he thought the old man
said — so he dashed to the
clubhouse to call an ambulance.
Much to the golfer's embarrassment,
there was nothing wrong with the
old man. It turned out that he
had said "Cart failure —!"

Etiquette. Use of Golf Cart

Local Rules governing the use of golf carts must be strictly observed.

In the 1938 U.S. Open at Cherry Hills
Country Club in Denver, Colorado,
Ray Ainlsey hit his ball into a creek
beside the 16th green. Instead of
taking a drop he tried to play it out
of the water. And tried and tried and
tried. He finally extricated the ball
and holed out for a championship-
record 19.

When your opponent is driving off you should stand where he can see you, but do not stand behind a player, or in such a position that he may be distracted.

Two Edinburgh golfers played a
unique match in 1848. They teed off
at Bruntsfield and played to the top
of Arthur's Seat, an 800 foot hill
which dominates the city.

Always play without undue delay and leave the putting green as soon as all the players in your group have holed out.

A ball driven off at the John O'Gaunt Club, Sutton, Bedfordshire, landed in London, 40 miles away! The ball actually landed in a passing vegetable lorry . . . and stayed there till it dropped out when the vegetables were being delivered to Covent Garden market in London.

Carefully replace any divots and smooth out footprints in bunkers.

In 1957 on Killarney golf course, a
player sliced his ball into a lake . . .
and it knocked out a fat trout rising
to catch a fly. The player's partner
waded in to retrieve the ball —
and the trout!

Etiquette. The Flagstick

Always replace the flagstick carefully in the hole in an upright position.

Playing with only a 3 iron Dick
Kimborough once completed a
round on the 6068 yards North Platte
course, Nebraska in 30 minutes
10 seconds.

Never hold up the players behind you. Invite faster groups to play through.

Finding his ball buried in a grassy
bunker at Hale, Cheshire, in 1935,
A.M. Chevalier played with a
niblick . . . and three balls came
shooting out, only for all of them to
fall back into the bunker, coming to
rest within a foot of each other.

Do not play your ball until any players ahead of you have moved out of range of your shot.

At Koolan Island Golf Club in Western
Australia, the 6th hole is also used as
the town's airstrip. A local rule states
that "Aircraft and vehicular traffic
have right of way at all times."

Players should ensure that any electronic device taken on to the course does not distract other players

Lossiemouth golf course in the north of Scotland is very close to an air station and in June 1971 Martin Robertson's drive form the 9th tee hit a Royal Navy jet as it came in to land. Fortunately no damage was done to the plane though it was not reported if Martin recovered his ball.

You should always leave the golf course in the condition in which you expect to find it.

AND FINALLY . . .

Me and Gnasher have had loads of laughs showing you how **NOT** to play golf.

OK, we got most of the Rules wrong first time, but now we've got the hang of them we'll stick to the right way from now on.

Menaces always play fair 'n' square, you know. It's best to stick to the Rules.

Got to go now — I'm teeing off against Desperate Dan from The Dandy in ten minutes.

Fetch my crash helmet, Gnasher — that cowboy's one wild hitter . . .

A copy of the Rules of Golf can be obtained from
The R & A website at www.randa.org or by calling
the Rules of Golf order line: +44 (0)1924 245416